Orangutan Houdini

LAUREL NEME

Illustrated by

KATHIE KELLEHER

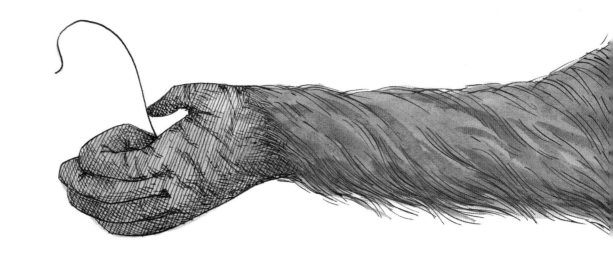

To Chris and Jackson, the loves of my life—LN

For my wonderful girls–Kelley and Skyler—KK

www.bunkerhillpublishing.com
Bunker Hill Publishing, Inc.
285 River Road, Piermont
New Hampshire 03779, USA

10 9 8 7 6 5 4 3 2 1

Library of Congress Control Number: 2013957794

ISBN: 978-1-59373-153-3
e-book ISBN: 978-1-59373-176-2

Designed by JDL
Printed in China

Fu Manchu, a twelve-year-old male orangutan, slipped a biscuit through the metal bars. His neighbor, an obese female named Heavy Lamar, snatched the cookie and stuffed it into her mouth.

Fu held out a second biscuit.

Heavy reached for it but Fu pulled away and looked up at the top of Heavy's pen, where wires for a light fixture crossed the dingy concrete.

Fu offered the treat again and stared at the ceiling. The message was clear. Fu wanted a swap.

The portly ape stretched up, stripped off a metal strand, and presented it to Fu.

Fu grinned, as only an orangutan can, and slipped his furry orange fingers through the bars for the exchange.

The sun glinted through the trees as Fu headed for the moat separating his enclosure from the outside world. He shared his pen with four orangutans: his mate Tondalayo; a stout older female named Sophia; and two adolescents—Toba (a female) and Dennis (a male). On warm autumn days like this, his zookeepers opened the outdoor area for the animals to play, something Fu normally enjoyed.

Today, however, Fu had other ideas.

The gangly ape scampered down the air vent louvers and scurried to the door cut into the wall of the dry trench. Fu glanced around and slipped his long fingers inside his mouth.

With his back toward the viewing area, he tugged at the bottom of the door with his left hand and, with his right, fiddled with the lock. A minute later, the door popped open.

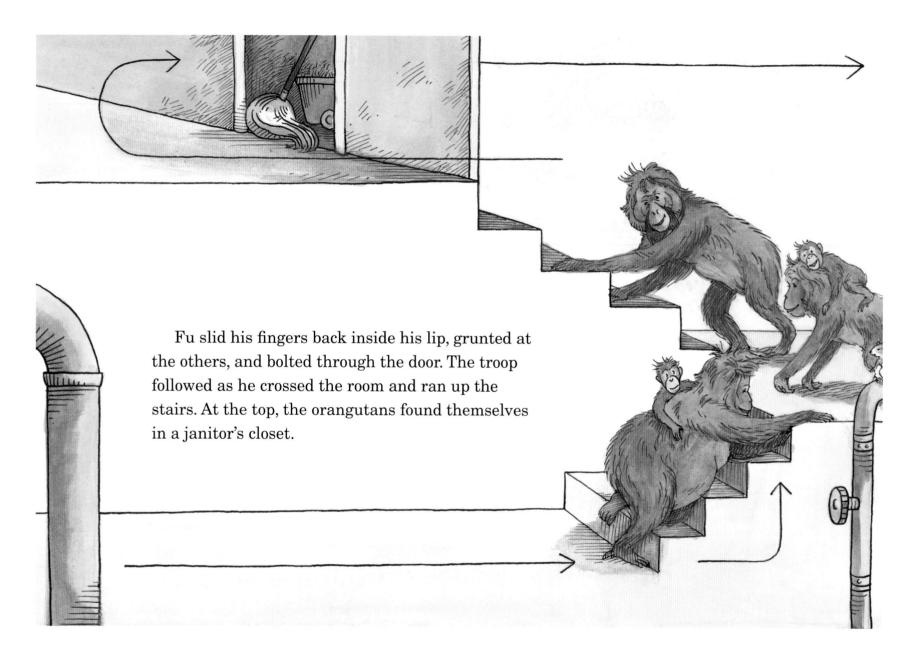

Fu slid his fingers back inside his lip, grunted at the others, and bolted through the door. The troop followed as he crossed the room and ran up the stairs. At the top, the orangutans found themselves in a janitor's closet.

Bumping into a mop, Fu turned the door handle. He entered the foyer, crossed the lobby, and pushed open a set of glass doors leading outside to the rest of the zoo.

Fu squinted in the sunshine and quickly discovered the perfect spot to spend the morning: a stand of elm trees on a hill above the elephant corral.

He darted to the small grove and climbed hand-over-foot and foot-over-hand up one of the trees.. As he planted himself in a crook between two branches, his family settled in nearby. Below, two elephants barely noticed the five balls of red fur dotting the trees.

Fu's tranquility didn't last long.

In the distance, head zookeeper Jerry Stones scolded his staff.

"How could you be so careless?" Jerry yelled. "Which one of you forgot to close and lock the door?"

Fu listened to the angry voice. He knew what was coming and wasn't surprised when Jerry arrived at the foot of his tree an hour later.

Fu liked Jerry. He'd known him for years. The zookeeper always treated him with kindness and ensured that his every need was met. Jerry never tolerated misbehavior. The man had a knack for anticipating Fu's antics and usually stopped them before they could start.

But not this time.

Jerry was smart. But Fu was smarter.

Jerry stood at the base of the tree and cooed. Fu pretended he didn't notice. The large ape ripped a small handful of leaves. He glanced down and placed one on his tongue.

Jerry sighed. He climbed the trunk and offered the orangutan his hand.

In reality, Fu didn't mind going back. He'd achieved his goal . . . and knew he could escape anytime he wanted.

Fu touched Jerry's hand and headed down the tree.

The next warm day, about a week later, Fu couldn't resist—not that he tried. Again, he climbed down the louvered air vents into the moat and headed straight for the furnace room door. He spit into his hand, pulled back the door with brute force, and fiddled until the lock unlatched.

He and the other orangutans scurried across the boiler room, darted up the stairs and twisted the knob of the final barrier to liberty.

Again, Fu and his family clambered up the trees near the elephant barn, where they munched on leaves and again relished the view.

It didn't take long until Jerry found the missing band of delinquents in the elms. From a distance, they looked like orange grapes on a half-eaten stem.

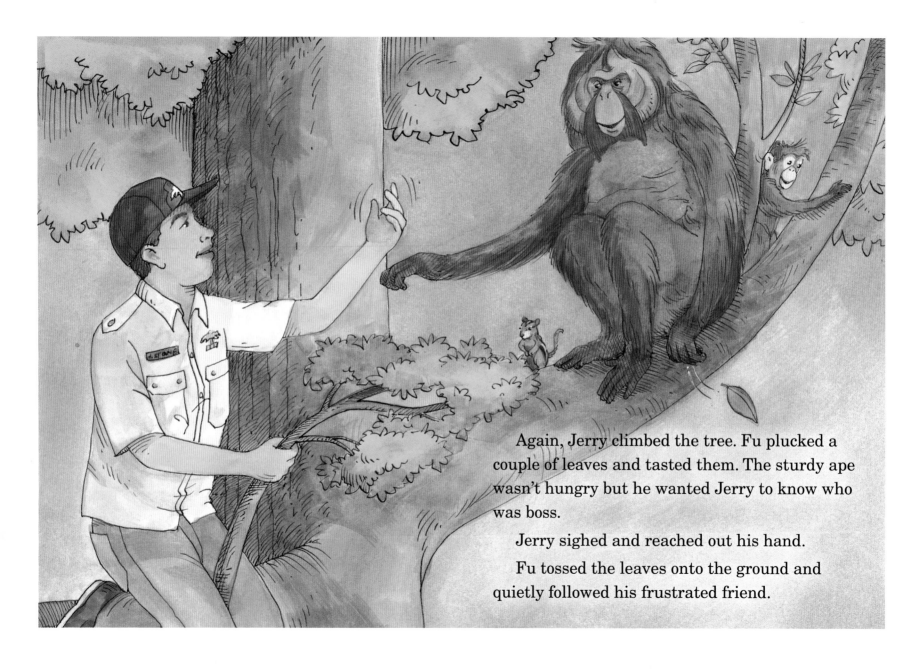

Again, Jerry climbed the tree. Fu plucked a couple of leaves and tasted them. The sturdy ape wasn't hungry but he wanted Jerry to know who was boss.

Jerry sighed and reached out his hand.

Fu tossed the leaves onto the ground and quietly followed his frustrated friend.

Back in their enclosure, Fu and the other orangutans watched Jerry and his staff double-check the dead bolts. Jerry was certain someone had forgotten to lock the door.

But the extra effort wouldn't help.

A few days later, Fu and his family again enjoyed the morning sun high atop the elms near the elephant pen. Fu liked seeing the huge mammals go about their daily routine.

When Jerry arrived, Fu took it in stride. He had known it was coming.

Again, he followed the zookeeper back to the enclosure without any fuss.

As soon as Jerry locked the orangutans back in their area, Fu heard the commotion.

"I'll fire the person responsible!" Jerry bellowed at his staff.

The keepers stood silently. Nobody would admit making a mistake.

But the reprimand spurred action. Desperate to keep their jobs, the zoo staff organized themselves into shifts to spy on the orangutans like undercover agents.

The next sunny day, Jerry's pager beeped.
"Come quick," one of this staff said.

Jerry rushed to their position, and one of the "spies" handed him binoculars. Jerry's mouth dropped open as he saw Fu fiddle with the lock and disappear through the furnace room door.

Over the next few weeks, Jerry changed the apes' routine.

"Fu's crafty," Jerry told his staff. "Pick up anything, you think, he could use to open that door!"

So, after the zoo closed each evening, the keepers scoured the pen. They crawled over every inch on their hands and knees and picked up every stick and stem that might become a tool for Fu.

But the strategy didn't work.

Fu and his friends escaped again . . . and again.

Finally, Jerry decided he had only one option: move the orangutans to a new—and more secure—enclosure.

When it was ready, Fu followed his friend down the corridor to his new home. The orangutan smiled a wide smile. A bit of silver glinted in the light.

"What was that?" Jerry wondered, pulling down Fu's lip to look inside.

Fu stuck his stuck his fingers inside his mouth and handed Jerry his treasure: a four-inch piece of wire bent into a horseshoe shape that fit perfectly around the ape's gum.

The deception was over, but only because Fu wanted it to be.

The rest of his days, Fu enjoyed his new surroundings.

He also relished his newfound acclaim as an honorary member of the American Association of Locksmiths.

AUTHOR'S NOTE:

While the main events of this story are true, some details are guesses.

Fu Manchu's escapes first occurred in October 1968 at the Henry Doorly Zoo in Omaha, Nebraska. The escapes included here were not his first. Fu used to open up his chain-link fence and let everybody out. He'd also twist off padlocks, forcing staff to use heavy-duty models and cover them with stainless-steel plates. Typically, after an escape, Fu would sit by the building and wait for his keepers.

Other zoo orangutans have also escaped, including Karta at Australia's Adelaide Zoo and Ken Allen at the San Diego Zoo, who had his own fan club.

These escapes provide insights into the cognitive ability and intelligence of orangutans. In the classic book *Animal Tool Behavior*, primatologist Benjamin Beck compared tool use among the great apes. He noted that, if a screwdriver was left in a cage, a gorilla would ignore it, a chimpanzee would use it for everything but its intended purpose, while an orangutan would notice it immediately "but ignore it lest a keeper discover the oversight." If the tool remained unnoticed, the orangutan would wait until night and then pick the locks or dismantle the cage and escape.

Escapes like Fu's demonstrate an orangutan's ability to deceive, which shows significant mental abilities. Fu had to understand Jerry's behavior and predict that, if Jerry found the wire, the keeper would take it away. He then had to decide to outwit Jerry and devise a plan to conceal the tool. That meant Fu had to analyze potential hiding places given Jerry's likely behavior and reject those that were too risky.

Fu also had to "reverse-engineer" the lock and design a tool to open it. With that design in mind, he needed to obtain the necessary materials and construct it in a way that would work and that he could hide from view.

Fu was special to all who knew him. When young, he would slide inside a keeper's parka, wiggle his arms down the sleeves (so that both were inside) and then play with the keeper. When older, he would take his keepers' hands and make them pat their heads, rub their bellies, and slap their faces.

Fu never hurt a soul. On at least three separate occasions, he rescued keepers who were getting chewed up or bitten by attacking orangutans. He also saved a curator who, while trying to catch a young orangutan, slipped on the wet floor. The curator stuck out his hand for balance and inadvertently put it inside an electrified plate-glass window. (The glass was electrified to prevent the orangutans from finger-painting on it.) As the man lay on the floor, Fu made sure he was okay and then took the man's right index finger and ran it down the three-quarter-inch bare strip between the glass and the frame, the one place that could be touched without harm—as if showing him how to avoid future problems.

For years, the Henry Doorly Zoo displayed Fu's American Association of Locksmiths honorary membership plaque on the wall as a tribute to the ape's ingenuity.

His antics have been documented in books and articles, including Eugene Linden's *The Parrot's Lament* and *The Octopus and the Orangutan*; Aline Alexander Newman's *Ape Escapes*; "Can Animals Think?" in *Time* (August 29, 1999); and "Animal Minds" on WNYC's *Radiolab* (January 25, 2010).

Fu eventually moved to the Gladys Porter Zoo in Brownsville, Texas, not because of his escapes but to prevent hybridization. (Fu was a Sumatran orangutan, and the others were Bornean.) Jerry moved to that same zoo where he is currently facilities director.

Fu Manchu passed away in the late 1990s.

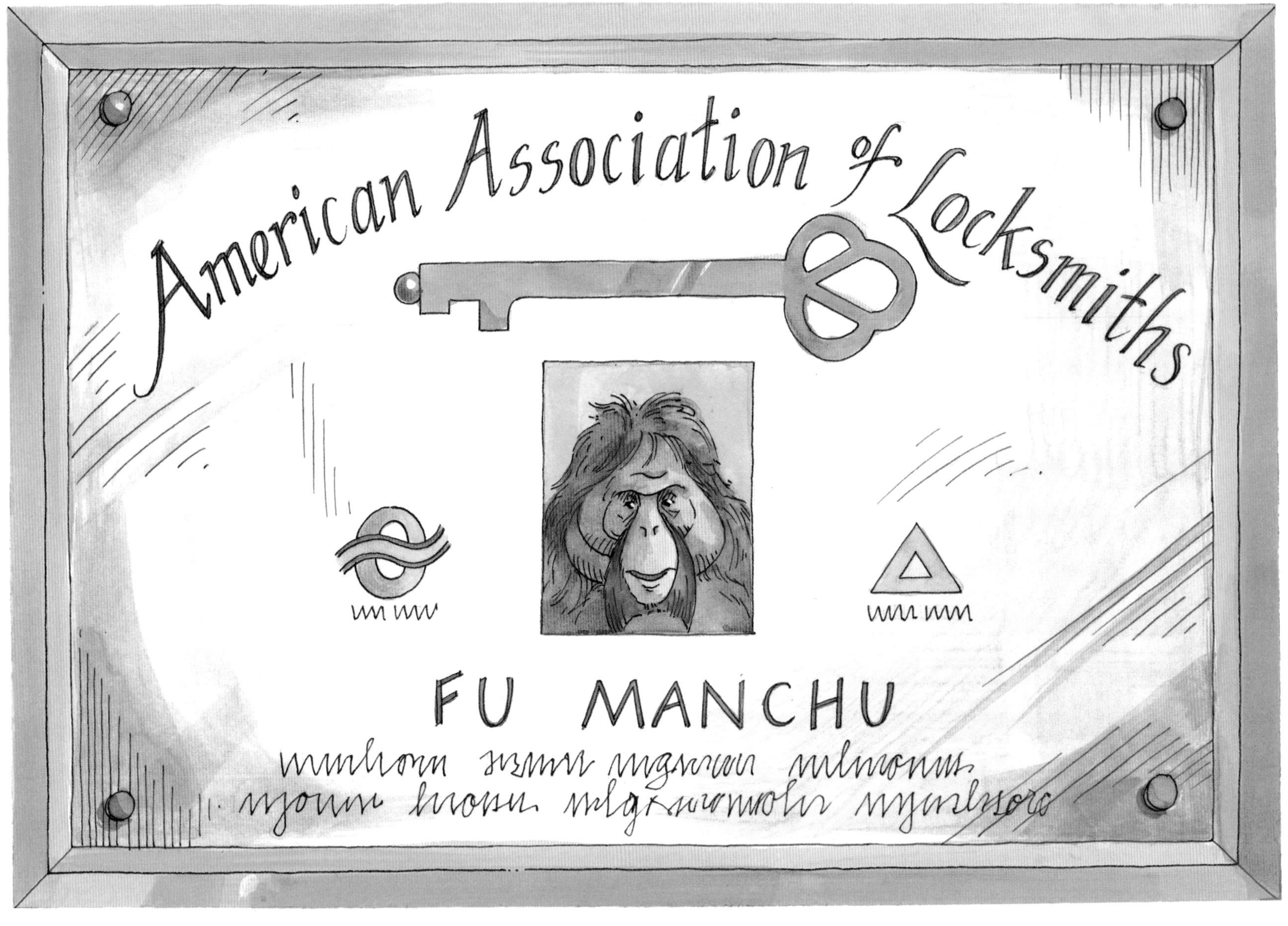
American Association of Locksmiths
FU MANCHU